To my two sons, Matthew and Daniel who have been the pinnacle of my life as it has played out in my own personal playing fields. They unleashed a love within me I didn't even know I had.

To

dearest Heather

MARY MALLIA

Playing Fields

Happy Birthday!

What a treat it's been sharing space, energy, life experience, laughs and cries – you're one in a million!

Much love,
Mary

18/9/2025.

This book was professionally typeset on Reedsy.
Find out more at reedsy.com

Contents

Prologue

The world is changing ever so rapidly
   everything transforming ever so quickly.
   Can we keep up with the pace of progress,
   veiled in such misery pain and loneliness?

Here we take on some of life's darker themes
   and frame them in sepia - in black 'n' white,
   some pages seem somewhat harder to read
   putting what's been hidden in plain sight …

For these a courage is required
   a gumption to perceive it all,
   the poignant darkness all around,
   in the big things and the small.

Iridescent colour beams through others,
   verses like the sun bedazzling bright,
   bringing joy, bliss, solace and peace
   filling your being with sheer delight.

And in some like a meditation
   we enter into a contemplation,
   observing from the page's safety
   the sourness of each travesty

unfolding before our very eyes
beholding of the dark, its size -
at times touched by its rawness
evoking a sense of uneasiness;
at others a glimmer of peace
descends in a sense of ease,
silently shrouded in hope -
even if not knowing the scope
of what is going on right now,
knowing we'll make it through somehow.
Each poem has a tale to tell.
Please enjoy! I wish you well.

I

Part One

The Children

"Are you coming out to play later today?"
We always asked each other every day,
after we had finished school -
it used to be so ethereally cool.

Chapter 1

Lovers in the flesh

I suddenly hear a knock at the front door
   and a shuffle in the garden, furthermore.
   Who is it at this ungodly time,
   who disturbs my evening fine?

The second knock is louder still,
   I wait behind the door until,
   there is a gap, a silent space,
   and I shout, just in case …

My visitor is deaf, for
   the knocks at the door
   sounded very loud and urgent.
   I ask: "Who is it lady or gent?"

The reply comes in a gentle laugh,
   sounding like a smirk and a half.
   Slowly, I open the front door.
   Looking like never before -
   stood a tall and smart man,

"Guess who I am, if you can!"

Was I asleep or was I awake -
    I couldn't tell for goodness' sake!
    This gentleman did familiar seem -
    I still wasn't sure if this were a dream.
    The man I did recognise tall, smart,
    furtive, cheeky glances at him I dart.
    As if reading my mind,
    he comes in from behind
    the plant standing in the hallway,
    "I'd love to come in, if I may."

"You are already in," I replied,
    as a deep excited sigh I sighed.
    I ask if we had ever met.
    "Yes," he said, "on a TV set.
    You played the mother divine,
    I pretended you were mine.
    Do you remember this incident,
    which I'm sure wasn't an accident?"

I glared at the gentleman stood before me
    trying to get some sort of clarity.
    My mind befuddled,
    my body muddled -
    as this man they could not recall,
    although handsome and very tall.

He moved towards me,
    slowly and seductively.

Was this the part we had played,
were love and passion displayed?
He looked tender and compassionate,
peaceful, loving and rather passionate.
We hugged and kissed
my lips he just missed,
so we brushed cheek against cheek
as my knees wobbled and went weak
he continued to move closer to me.
What would his next step be?

My heart fluttered
as my mouth muttered
a few sweet nothings in his ear
I shouted, so he could hear.

Still not sure if awake or asleep -
does here illusion, reality meet?
What will his next move be,
would it prove his identity?

Should I have let a stranger come in
to my house, on an impulsive whim?
He does seem strangely familiar so,
I decided to go with the flow.

My heart likes his vibration warm,
my mind - my heart tries to warn:
"Are you sure this is what you desire,
he seems to be wildly on fire?"

My heart reassures my mind,
  it does him very handsome find
  and since the feeling is mutual
  I perform the forthcoming ritual.

A long red silken sari I wear.
  I've had it a very long time, I swear!
  He unwraps me slowly and seductively,
  at my naked body he gazes lovingly.

Little bits appearing one at a time,
  intrigued he remarks: "Your skin does shine
  and smells of sweet-smelling scented flowers
  and feels as refreshing as fresh April showers."

I coyly look into his ocean blue eyes,
  and say what he says is very nice.
  Slowly I slide onto the beckoning bed -
  from here onwards, enough's been said.
  Our bodies entwined, smouldering with heat,
  moving as one from our head to our bare feet
  we rumbled
  and tumbled
  in total abandon,
  an act so seemingly random.

His languid kiss melted all my fears.
  His gentle caress moved me to tears.
  Is this man human or from another dimension?
  His touch so light 'n' tender, I forgot to mention.
  It made me wonder whence he had come

and how so suddenly we seemed to be one.
How can I explain how he made me feel,
still asking myself if this is really for real.
Is he man or an angel divine,
is this reality or a dream of mine?

His touch came as light as a feather
 caressing me all over and whether
 it were a dream or whether not -
 my whole being was very hot.

In his warm embrace
 tensions melted
 bodies sweltered
 hearts sheltered
 going with the flo
 in the present mo
 passions flying
 fears dying -
 souls expanding
 nothing demanding
 spirits upward ascend
 heavenly roses' scent
 like a sweet perfume
 filling the entire room.

Suddenly he is there no more.
 Had he bolted for the door?
 This new union - being as one,
 ended before it had even begun!

On the floor he left a tiny white feather,
   awake, asleep, man, angel, whether -
   He left as suddenly as he had come,
   bereft my body feels slightly numb.
   How could he so heedlessly go?
   That's what I really wanted to know.

The feather whispered softly in my ear:
   "He isn't gone, dear, he's very near!"
   I looked around and couldn't see,
   where he had taken himself to be.
   I feel a freshly blowing breeze,
   and suddenly I begin to sneeze.

I come falling into the room with a bump,
   and crash onto the floor with a thump.
   The feather I pick up from the floor,
   as the dream, is a dream no more.

Chapter 2

Lovers in Spirit

Are you here my darling,
   in spirit and in truth?
   I am your presence awaiting
   your dearest, darling Ruth.

I am here waiting Ruth,
   my dearest darling sweet'art,
   can't wait to hold you in my arms
   and into the sunset off we dart.

My dearest darling David
   I have waited for so long -
   ensconced in this sweet embrace,
   our bodies dancing to our song.

My sweetest darling sweetheart Ruth,
   my being for you languidly longs -
   to be caressed by your smooth skin is,
   like being touched by heavenly throngs.

My dearest darling David
  can you hear my being pine,
  then as you gently approach me,
  it suddenly begins to shine?

My sweetest darling Sweetheart,
  my old heart skips a beat,
  when your elusive image in dreams
  comes to me in my sleep.

My dearest darling David
  like ships passing in the night,
  your visions of me in dreams,
  I hope fill you with delight.

Oh gentlest, sweetest darling Ruth
  I relish these visions sweet -
  I cannot contain myself with joy,
  with the anticipation of when we meet.

Oh dearest darling David
  I am gladly reassured
  that our meeting has been planned
  soon, by the heavens procured.

Oh dearest darling David
  I do not intend to tease,
  our real encounter on the Earth plane
  we must ASAP release!

Oh sweetest, gentlest darling Ruth

How can this come to be?
How can you make dreams come true?
I humbly ask of thee.

Oh dearest darling David
  it's all been written down -
  take heart and do not be sad,
  quickly wipe away that frown.

Oh sweetest, gentlest darling Ruth
  I am so very happy
  that one day very soon
  you shall come to me.

Oh dearest darling David
  it's the other way around.
  I heard through the grapevine
  I shall need to be found.

Oh sweetest, gentlest darling Ruth
  where do I begin
  to look throughout the Earth,
  with-out and within?

Oh dearest darling David
  make sure you follow your nose
  it's not a very small one
  and great at smelling, I suppose!

Oh sweetest, gentlest darling Ruth
  isn't that a bit rude?

Teasing me about my nose,
is that not rather crude?

I imagine you like an angel
    swanning in the air -
    remarking on the size of my nose,
    I don't think that that's fair!

Oh dearest darling David
    I don't mean to be mean
    I do like teasing quite a bit
    not meaning to demean.

Oh sweetest, gentlest darling Ruth
    I guess that you are right
    my nose is a bit out of joint,
    yet I hope you like my height.

Oh dearest darling David
    Your height is a great gift,
    for when I can't reach the top
    up high, you can me lift.

Oh sweetest, gentlest darling Ruth
    I might be tall and handsome,
    but to lift you up sky-high
    I might demand a ransom!

Oh dearest darling David
    what if I offer you my heart?
    What if I promise that my love,

14

from you shall never depart?

Is that enough a ransom
   offered in exchange, for
   being lifted up so high?
   I can't offer any more.

Oh sweetest sweetheart Ruth,
   what more can I expect?
   That makes me a happy man,
   your loving heart I will protect.

You won't just reach the wardrobe
   or get stars from up in the sky,
   I shall lift you up inside yourself
   our temperatures shall run high!

This lifting up business
   to the heavens and above -
   akin to flying in the spirit,
   soaring spirits in Love.

And after we have met in spirit,
   I hope we meet in the flesh.
   I look forward to our encounter,
   the anticipation of it, I relish.

Oh dearest darling David
   this dream is nearing its end.
   Will you to my expectant heart,
   a little message and sign send?

15

Chapter 3

Mistaken Identity

A little black cat it is
　　who comes to sit
　　on her sofa
　　on her bed.

"Who are you?" Gloria asks,
　　whilst in its warmth, she basks.
　　"What is your name?
　　You just came
　　out of nowhere,
　　it suddenly seems
　　like in surreal dreams.
　　Are you for real and true?
　　Feels like I've always known you."

The little black cat,
　　as it sat
　　on her sofa
　　on her bed
　　on her lap

made itself at home.

For a while
    Loneliness smiled,
    as it came inside
    warming her house
    with its love.
    When it suddenly departed,
    Loneliness started
    to feel sad again.

The next day, it purred outside her door,
    with a great sense of urgency, whats more.
    Gloria quickly ushered it inside,
    from the cold cruel world to hide.
    "You're always welcome here, my dear,"
    she whispered softly in its chewed bloody ear.

Had it been in a fight,
    come to her in flight
    for shelter -
    from the cold outside.
    Had it come here to hide?

They play, they cuddle and they kiss.
    Afraid that its affection she'll miss,
    Gloria puts all chores to one side
    and allows it to sit beside
    her, as she writes
    and busily types
    a verse or two

17

about you
Smartie.

For in her inquiries
    in answer to her queries,
    she is told his name is *Smartie.*
    He is *male* they say to her, verily.

So, a male black cat
    called Smartie
    's, been visiting Gloria
    almost every day,
    come what may.

Sometimes he would miss a day or two
    but, that's OK for Gloria knew
    in time he would be back,
    purring outside her front door
    wanting a cuddle, and what's more
    a little affection and a play -
    easing the loneliness of the day.
    Her days were lonely no more,
    since Smartie's miaowing at her door.
    She looked forward in anticipation
    to his purrs,
    'nd fluffy tail
    molting all over
    the floor
    the sofa
    the bed
    her lap.

Smartie, her faithful and constant friend,
   changed Gloria's world in an instant.
   The moment he knocked at her door
   she wasn't lonely anymore.
   A new lease on life he gave her,
   she loved having him there.

Her days turned upside down,
   Smartie wiped away each frown,
   he put a smile on her saddened face,
   filling her days with joyful grace.
   Was he that powerful a cat
   that as it on her sofa sat
   her mood it changed
   sadness exchanged
   for joy in her bones
   singing celestial tones,
   blissfully filling Gloria
   with a heavenly euphoria?

She was surprised to learn
   and had to slowly discern
   how Smartie, it turns out -
   shall'll have to whisper, not shout,
   is a female cat, not a male.

Do her owners not know
   that their cat is female, so
   their cat Smartie,
   is a she and not a *he*?
   Has she ever sat

19

on their lap
for a nap?
Or on their bed
joyfully curled
quietly purred
caressing her fluff,
calling *his* bluff?

For *he* is a she,
    couldn't they see?
    And *his* gracious hostess Gloria,
    thought she'd name her Victoria.

Chapter 4

Victoria

"I got suddenly and rudely taken -
   my warmth and comfort crudely shaken.
   Why was Gloria picking me up,
   handing me to that woman who wouldn't shut up?
   To a woman who loves me not, she handed me
   over, to a woman with whom I didn't want to be.

For to her a mere beast I am, a pest,
   no feelings, thoughts or at best
   an animal with no rights,
   always getting into fights
   which I was not, of course,
   that is all a lie - sadly false.

Her ginormous angry dog *Belle*
   is not - it's ugly - and a hell
   of a beastly carnivorous canine
   its outward countenance benign,
   but I know deep inside its wrath
   seeks to turn me into broth.

My ears she chews
  and my chin too.
  My eyes she grazes,
  to mention but a few,
  of the injuries she inflicts,
  intentionally to hurt and scar,
  growling I hear her from afar.
  I have to seek refuge elsewhere.
  I stay at Gloria's - I love it there.

This youngish, friendly new lady I seek
  I remember the first time we did meet.
  She called to me from by the pavement,
  I went to her making a clear statement
  that overwhelmingly pleased to see her I was,
  as I rolled onto my belly and purred, I suppose.

I remember when I saw her that very first time,
  it seemed as if she'd been an owner of mine.
  Perhaps, in another life, another setting,
  I lay on my back enjoying her gentle petting
  as she stroked me whispering words caring, kind.
  Wow, it was amazing! Do you think I did mind?
  No, I was overwhelmingly above the moon,
  that my prayers shall all be answered soon,
  I should be able to go to her homely house,
  laying, eating, resting, as quiet as a mouse.
  I promised her I won't be any trouble at all
  there I shall take refuge - life 'll be a ball!
  As Gloria is a kind-hearted loving soul
  on whom life has sadly taken its toll

welcomed me into her life with joy,
to her, a brand new friend to enjoy,
to play with, and have some fun
a new life for her and I'd begun.

The friendship which suddenly ensued
is now sadly being carefully reviewed,
as I end up back in my *real* owners' abode
I am not happy, it must be emphatically told!
They lock me up inside a very tiny cage -
my owner's husband overflowing with rage,
at me having sought out my own sanctuary,
in their tiny world - the biggest travesty.

How dare *their* cat fight for its right
to seek its own owner, and for this right fight?
How dare *their* cat whose sex they did not know,
its love and affection on another bestow?
How dare *their* pet which they neglected, be set
on being adopted by a stranger, this they won't let
happen – not over their dead bodies they swore -
as a demeanour ferocious and vicious they wore.

I have to find a way my sweet Gloria to warn
for they regard her with the greatest of scorn.
They definitely do not wish her well,
this, to her I must promptly tell.
They are keeping me locked up inside
but, here inside I shall not long reside.
I shall find a way to escape soon,
go and tell Gloria of this doom.

23

Gloria must be waiting worriedly for me,
looking for me, when me she doesn't see.
She must have got my bowl of food ready,
dried food and fresh water for my brekkie.
She must be calling my name out loud
but outside, at this mo I'm not allowed.
Gloria I shall have to find a way to tell,
but how if locked up in a cold prison cell?
She shall come and rescue me very soon I hope
otherwise, with this enslavement I mightn't cope.
Without the love of my Gloria sweet,
how can I the day in joyful wonder greet?

My ardent prayer to God sacred, God divine
's returning to Gloria in her warm sunshine,
returning to the comfort of her house,
where I shall sit as quiet as a mouse."

Gloria
"Victoria, Victoria, I am so sorry
I am weary and sick with worry.
I carried you to *her* who is not nice,
my apologies alone will not suffice.
I shall have to find a way to set you free,
from her viciously evil tyranny.

I can hear you miaowing as if by my door,
I open, and you are there no more.
I look at the gate
at half past eight.
Still, you are not there.

24

I wait - vacantly stare -
hoping you've now been set free
and running back gleefully to me.

But, so far you have not.
  Guilt inside me does rot,
  inside me, it does ferment -
  I did put up a fight and an argument,
  making clear my outright sentiment
  that I did not want to let you go,
  in my house you're welcome. So,
  she did not like my assertive stance,
  now I can only love you from a distance.
  She said repeatedly you were *her* cat -
  it doesn't seem like it, from where I'm sat.

You chose to come to me
  to share good times and company,
  our times were full of cheerful chatter
  it seemed like nothing else did matter.
  I loved getting you some good food to eat,
  as your tummy rumbled – it needed meat
  and some other food for nourishment,
  for this, you are locked up as punishment.

I feel very guilty as I should've let her shout
  for you from your refuge to slowly come out.
  I shouldn't have so simply handed you to her,
  so sorry to have done that, my bad - I err
  and ask for forgiveness for this of you.
  Do you think this you can give me, to

ease my guilt and sense of shame?
You are innocent. I'm to blame."

Victoria

"When she came to collect me
   she was very arrogant and rude,
   I heard her hoarse harsh command.
   How could she have been so crude?

Threatening to sue you, is what she does best
   as *her* little cat Victoria flees the nasty nest
   and silently seeks refuge elsewhere -
   How dare she? She thinks it's unfair.

She believes that because me at times she feeds
   and to own and control me she avidly needs,
   that I belong to her and to her family.
   Do I want to be a part of her travesty?

NO - I DO NOT! And on that note I say,
   her and her soul-destroying edicts I shan't obey.
   Her desire to coerce, control and destroy me,
   is evident for you and everybody else to see!

I shall find a way out of this imprisonment
   to everybody's sheer astonishment!
   As a very powerful and creative cat am I,
   I shan't take it lying down and die.
   I shall fight for my freedom with all my zeal

my true strength and power I shall reveal,
I shall make sure she knows I set myself free,
so back with my sweet little Gloria I can be.
I shall not hover or languidly hang about
but, swiftly go to her door and shout:

"Gloria, Gloria,
   my sweet warrior -
   Do not worry, do not fret,
   one thing, do not forget!

There is nothing to forgive
   for as long as I shall live,
   I'll remember your kindness and generosity too -
   I know you love me – and I will always love you!' "

Chapter 5

Two Black Cats

A blue velvet sofa I used to own.
    Two black cats sat on this stately throne,
    two furry bodies warming the grand seat
    where both cuteness and cheekiness meet.

They sit languidly, whilst I busily bustle,
    Rosie intently peering at leaves as they rustle
    yet, choosing to stay in the warm cosy room,
    whilst she does herself, meticulously, groom.

Pepsi, on the other hand, loves the great outdoors,
    prowling outside, fighting territory wars.
    She firmly stands her ground,
    stealthily sneaking around.

They love hunting down the odd bird or two,
    a present for me - which I misconstrue -
    for a being has been suddenly shaken,
    its poor life unsuspectingly taken.

Given to me as a gift from Pepsi,
   in great reverence and generosity.
   Rosie would join in the fun,
   chasing until that battle's won.

Playing copycats
   catching rats
   contentedly purr
   velvety black fur
   serenely sleeping
   languidly leaping
   hunting hungrily
   playing playfully
   felines feeding
   not much needing.

Oh how I wish, how I wish, I were a cat,
   sat silently snugly on a soft cosy mat,
   or on a comfy sofa in the sun,
   impervious to everything, everyone.
   Unaware of trouble, toil and strife,
   oblivious to tragedies and to life's
   diseases, deaths, blinding illusions -
   sleeping profoundly through fatal delusions.

Chapter 6

Angela and Mary

I stopped to speak to Angela
   on my way back from my walk.
   We warmly exchanged greetings,
   when a robin nearby began to talk ...

"Dearest Angela and Mary
   you two women both so dear,
   it's so nice to stop and chat,
   that's why I'm stopping here.

I love to see you both smile,
   as you greet each other now.
   Oh, how I love it when you
   humans connect – it's wow!

For I know you only met,
   one other time before.
   Mary you were walking past,
   Angela you were by your door.

It was a hasty meeting
    there was lots of commotion,
    Today's calm connection,
    set a new friendship in motion.

It's just so lovely and refreshing
    to watch grown humans smile.
    Things are getting pretty hefty,
    I can't imagine why!

Creation from my point of view
    has always been so perfect.
    The law that binds us all in love,
    in our hearts does reflect …

The love of our divine Creator
    God's melodious work of art,
    Sacred and divine we are made,
    sacredness singing in our heart."

Chapter 7

Little Robin Red-Breast

I'm only a little robin red-breast
    but I know perfectly who I am
    I instinctively sing my heart out,
    as is for me life's very own plan.

I bring so much soul-solace
    to hearts lonely, spirits down,
    my singing bringing joy,
    turns into a smile, a frown.

Especially at Christmas time
    that very special time of year,
    when love, peace and jubilant joy
    replace war, anger, strife and fear.

My song from my heart is ushered
    filling my lungs, the whole of my chest
    and all the space for miles around me,
    north, south, east and west.

My greys do sometimes get me down,
   yet, my red I always wear with pride.
   All-in-all I am a robin red-breast,
   and my true colours I do not hide.

You couldn't see the red as clearly
   if the grey feathers weren't there.
   The grey isn't always celebrated,
   I don't think that that's fair.

I'm a little robin red-breast
   I know perfectly who I am
   I instinctively sing my heart out,
   as is for me life's very own plan.

Chapter 8

Doris and Helen

My dearest sister Helen,
   and my sister Doris too,
   time has not erased
   the love I have for you.

My dearest sister Helen,
   and my sister Doris too,
   you are always in my heart
   whatever you say or do.

My dearest sister Helen,
   and my sister Doris too,
   our paths now cross again.
   Oh! How I have missed you!

Your dearest sister Mary
   had not gone away,
   you won't get rid of her so easily,
   she is in your life to stay.

Her life we know 's been tricky
    Her suffering 's been great ,
    to meet up with you both one day
    she can hardly wait!

No end to her agonised anguish
    or to her endless poignant pain,
    but one day you shall all meet up
    come wind, hail, snow or rain.

And when you three all get together,
    Oh! How the heavens shall ring,
    everybody shall be able to hear
    heavenly choirs of angels sing.

They're singing of a reuniting
    of heaven's a simple soul,
    here on Earth sojourning
    as life tends to take its toll.

As you reunite in friendship,
    so do your life paths merge,
    and once again the power of love
    between you three shall re-emerge.

You do not need to meet in body,
    in spirit - that'll be fine,
    for when the good Shepherd comes, He says:
    "Come on in! You three are mine.

The enemy has tried to destroy

what I had so diligently planted,
he did his best to undo my work,
My artwork won't be supplanted.

I gather back my three little sheep,
returning to the fold they come.
I do not have a favourite among them,
for to me they are unique, yet one.

Each in their own way especially made
uniquely their life-purpose living out
yet, when the marching orders come
all three in unison shall begin to shout:

'We love you with all our might
our sacred divine Creator -
our sustainer, our life, our love, our light,
our Maker.
Whatever trifles life throws at us,
whether peace, harmony or discord,
a jubilant inner joy is always our reward
as we forge ahead in a faith unshakable,
with resolve and a courage unbreakable.

And each of us in our own little way
to our sacred Maker we humbly pray,
that our divine life-purpose we fulfill,
as divine sacred Creator's Will,
is etched upon our hearts, to love all,
we simply surrender to that sacred call.'"

It seems we have been separate
    yet, the whole time we've been apart,
    God has held each one of us in His bosom
    in the centre of His compassionate heart.

Chapter 9

Lindzi

Lindzi, Lindzi, Lindzi, Lindzi, Lindzi,
   dancing underneath the marquee
   in the midst of chaos and confusion,
   fighting with light to end the delusion
   that has taken hold of the human race,
   in the face of what's now taking place.

A courage she has patiently procured,
   in the face of evil steadily secured.
   Defiant to what is inherently wrong,
   despite persecution, dancing her song.
   A tune resplendent with the joy of life,
   a gladiatorial one, with a passion rife.

Truth her alibi in the midst of deceit
   exposing it unapologetically she does seek.
   Embodying truth with all her might,
   embracing what she knows is right;
   not putting her trust in institutions
   hoping they would find peaceful solutions.

She knows that they do not want peace;
   she exposes what media do not release.
   Lindzi vocalises her truth with a roar,
   with insurmountable courage and furore.
   From the ashes she is blightely arisen -
   free from the conditioned mind's prison.

When you have Lindzi as your friend
   with all under the sun you can contend,
   as she protects all those who are near,
   with a vengeance – courage - not fear.

Lindzi's a treasure of infinite worth,
   to endless works of art gives birth.
   For what her eyes see, her hands can make,
   giving new life to lifeless matter a new shape.

Co-creator with our Maker divine,
   from nothing creating patterns sublime
   transforming raw material into an objet d'art
   flooding from the creative love in her heart.

Within the spot on her forehead
   commonly called the *Third eye* -
   sharp, colourful, clairvoyant images,
   create visions of what is nigh.

The pictures on this canvas clear,
   are given to Lindzi, as she's the seer
   for those seeking the right path ahead,
   whether they're alive or whether they're dead.

A treasure so true -
    with gratitude – I thank you.
    This friendship's a true gift,
    my spirit it does uplift.

Chapter 10

Anna and Aileen

My dearest sister Anna
   your compassionate, gentle smile
   brings solace to us all and sundry,
   all the while... all the while...

My dearest sister Aileen
   I love it when you call.
   I relish our conversations,
   'bout the big things and the small.

My dearest sister Anna
   so sincere and so true,
   sharing an honest friendship with you
   I am well and truly grateful.

My dearest sister Aileen
   I love it when you smile,
   especially when on long walks we go
   mile ... after mile ... after mile ... .

My dearest sister Anna
    the roads from Russia to here,
    miles and miles so far away, they
    brought us together somehow, dear.

My dearest sister Aileen
    it's strange how our paths met.
    Bumping *coincidently* in Waitrose
    seems like it 'd been somehow set.

Anna, back to your cherished homeland,
    you took my beloved son -
    He loved it there, so much to learn,
    having also had such fun.

Both friendships rolled throughout the years,
    through life's inevitable ups and downs -
    changing moods, discussing foods,
    transforming into smiles, life's frowns.

My dearest sister Aileen
    I just wanted to say today,
    I shall always hold you in my heart
    come what may - come what may!

Your garden so pristinely pruned,
    Anya's sunflowers smiling in the sun.
    Finally, on this note I'd love to say,
    these friendships 're second to none!

Chapter 11

Lara

Her name is not Sara, Farah or Clara.
   No. Her beautiful name is Lara.
   I met her one sunny day on a walk
   and out of the blue we began to talk.

I love her purity
   shrouded so subtly,
   in her talk grounded in reality.
   I could feel my spirit stir,
   just there, where we were!
   Unpretentious and humble is she
   leaving a lot of peace within me,
   as she slowly walked away
   after we chatted, on that very first day,
   we both had found so much to say.

Her - wondering what to do for the best
   Me - talking of miracles and all the rest
   Her - gently and softly spoken
   Me - coarse yet, heart wide open

Her - tall, slim, slender and very kind
Me - shorter and stumpier you will find
Her - full of poise and grace
Me - smiling with food on my face!
Her - silken, long, straight hair
Me - curls blowing everywhere.

Since then this friendship grew,
    a seed that day was planted new,
    the tree has been generous and kind
    yielding dainty pink flowers, you will find.

Chapter 12

Patricia

Patricia we have wandered through the years
   together, amidst joys and torrents of tears
   spiritually holding each other's hand
   scribbling *I love you* in golden sand,
   gentle lapping waves these words do not erase,
   as we, upon this miracle in awe and wonder gaze
   your steadfast spirit me does inspire,
   seems like at times you are on fire.

Apart from when the flame runs low
   life beats the life out of the fire, so
   you stagger along the sandy beach,
   alone - that sacred space you reach,
   where the words *I love you* are written in the sand,
   here you pause – but, don't stop – it's not the end.

A heavenly vision comes to you from the sky
   and exactly how you cannot tell, or why,
   but a host of heavenly angels are seen
   where dark, black, menacing clouds had been.

Their heavenly symphony fills your being
your touch, your smell, your heart, your seeing.
Your soul dances to their angelic tune,
hoping it won't all suddenly end soon
your feet are lifted from off the ground
a new life and peace 're joyously found.
Your body shining through and through,
visible to me and experienced by you.
All worries and cares just melt away,
you ask the angels if they would stay.
They say they will, as the best's yet to come,
the Son is coming and bringing His mum,
the two are longing you to salute,
in great reverence and gratitude
for when alone in anguish and fear
alone in the dark you shed a tear,
they're both there with you dear.

They sometimes poke you with a nudge or two
to get your attention, without hurting you.
At times they send you a little white feather,
when the washing from the roof you gather.
These signs you sometimes ignore or miss,
"Now you must see them - we do insist!
For we have not left you to suffer alone,
your feet shan't be scorched nor hit a stone,
on turbulent water you shall confidently walk,
in foreign tongues to people, you shall talk,
as you proclaim God's sacred name on high,
His return is nigh! His return is nigh!"

The Son and His mum suddenly appear.
   The heavenly throng don't disappear
   but, its light becomes more intense
   filling you, Patricia, with confidence,
   your eyes uplifted into the sky,
   and now we know exactly why …

There strewn across the sky are many a shining star,
   some appear right close, others seem quite far.
   The Mother humbly dressed in white and blue,
   holding her beloved Son's hand as in He flew
   among the bright dazzling light -
   His body shining gold, silver white.
   Both Mother and Son sweetly smile,
   having waited for this moment for a while.

Patricia, you are in an ecstatic trance kneeling,
   heavenly peace, love and joy feeling,
   throughout your body, beyond and into space,
   filling you heart and soul with a divine grace.

Thoughts suspending
   Life never-ending
   Love divine
   Peace sublime
   Joyous smiles
   No lies -
   Jubilant tears
   No fears -
   Bright light
   Sheer delight

Light-body transforms
Transcending norms.

A joyous peace not as we humans know,
   only that which sacred Love does bestow
   fills you right up to the rim,
   overflowing from the brim -
   A taste of heaven you have seen,
   Patricia, to Heaven you have been.

Chapter 13

<u>The Way</u>

I don't need a recording to tell me
    anything I don't already know.
    I trust my own inner knowing,
    as my inner wisdom's growing.

We are inherently sacred and divine,
    our inner knowing, we must find,
    it is not in books called *holy writing*,
    nor in words someone else is citing.

It beats in the depths of our very own heart,
    its whispers reverberate within-without.
    Inscribed in silence, within our DNA,
    forever present - it doesn't decay.

Inside us codes that don't need decoding,
    as our souls and spirit knowing
    what these light-codes do mean,
    the way lighting they have been.

There seem to be too many theories floating about,
    from where they get their knowledge, I do doubt.
    Not sure it's my truth, that they are speaking,
    their words do not all resonate with meaning.

A cacophony of voices in my head explode,
    my own inner knowing seems to erode.
    I'm not sure if I'm coming or going -
    it's blurring my inherent inner knowing!

What lies within our own spirit, embodied,
    needs to be carefully examined and studied.
    Only accessible in stillness and silence....
    In Nature, in breathing, in quietening the busy mind,
    this inner wisdom and your true essence you will find.

Chapter 14

Captain Plugwash

I welcome you into my den of iniquity,
   established since the day of antiquity.
   Allow me to lull you in-
   to my vessel of slovenly sin.
   My tiny boat violently a' rocking,
   with my libido shaking, shocking!

I look back at the days of old.
   "You are good in bed," I had been told.
   Reassured that all the right spots I knew
   not needing a guide or a gentle cue,
   my fingers ran smoothly through lush terrain,
   luscious valleys, hills, all overflowing with rain.

Alas, now the valley has run dry.
   For the life of me, I don't know why.
   I seem to have lost that golden touch
   and perhaps try too hard - too much
   effort I put into leering, luring in
   innocent women, with silk olive skin.

I cannot comprehend what has gone wrong.
  My body's stopped singing its sensual song.
  My magic touch I have definitely lost
  dried up valleys, me now accost
  deserts of loneliness, dry terrain
  all formed due to a serious lack of rain.

I have now sadly run out of luck.
  And do you think I give a f**k?
  Of course I do, for heaven's sake,
  empty beds and bedrooms make
  me seem like an old stupid fool,
  who is always willing to drool
  over any pair of legs and bums
  as my libido frustratingly hums
  the tune of a sad old defunct man
  who would like to, but he can
  not -
  As functionality he has not got,
  of his most crucial body part -
  and by this, I don't mean the heart!
  I want to entice women into my *pleasure room*,
  I hope it will get moving and wake up soon.

I can't understand how they say *no*.
  I smile so my golden teeth show.
  I tell them, "I am good in bed,
  this is oft to me been said."
  Yet, slowly and deliberately they turn away,
  to my utter shock and sheer dismay.

52

Chapter 15

Mark

Mark,
    sailing through life like the Cutty Sark.
    Does he dance on his window-sill
    into the small hours, until
    the long-awaited sunrise,
    to everyone's sheer surprise?

An exceedingly kind and wonderful man,
    helping anyone, anytime he can.
    His love of animals, mostly cats,
    but not exclusively, includes rats.
    His demeanour warm and calm,
    to my vexed spirit, a gentle balm.

He was minding his own business, when one day
    I descended upon him, shall we say,
    as a nosy neighbour, a friendly soul
    to forge a friendship, my simple goal.
    I shook Mark's world to the core,
    as his peace and quiet was no more!

Early morning away from me he ran,
   into his blessed white Transit van.
   He said he was going to work to
   earn a living, but that's not true.
   Since I moved in next door last July,
   about his job he has had to lie.

He clambers out quietly every morning
   without heeding, without warning.
   Silently into his Transit van he goes,
   and where to, only heaven knows.
   Every morning he drives ahead,
   not really going to work, instead …

He aimlessly drives across some fields
   an exercise, which not much income yields,
   after that he walks into a nondescript shop,
   a particular shop, which makes one stop
   and wonder curiously, at what lay behind
   that old oak back door - what will one find?

Greeted warmly every morning, it seems by everyone
   is Mark, as through the back door he's seen to come.
   What lay behind that aged, oak wooden door
   all want to know, as mysteriously Mark for
   ages into the ether oddly disappears,
   hours later, he mysteriously reappears.

Where he goes,
   nobody knows.
   He lands deftly on his feet,

while his clients he hurries to meet.
Some see him and some do not, of course,
yet, to his gentle presence all have recourse.

He never knows on the day,
which assignment's coming his way.
Will it be a saddened widow black,
needing someone with whom to chat?
Or a lonely wife, or a mother bereft,
all her loved ones gone, no-one's left?
Will it be an elderly man,
Charlie, Dave, Peter or Dan
feeling isolated in his cold room
hoping someone will visit soon?
Or is it a young lively lad,
well turned-out, smartly clad,
who's been abused by a community member,
trying to forget and not remember -
drowning his sorrow in alcohol and drugs,
his smart suit seeming more like rugs?
Or is it a black cat waiting to be fed,
to play and rest on a warm soft bed?

The list is endless, assignments vary -
yet Mark's always cheerful, never weary.
He takes it all in his stride,
a mind open and heart wide
full of compassion, gentle, kind
whatever the assignment, he doesn't mind.
He always smiles first,
to satiate their thirst

for a friendly face,
or just in case -
they needed someone to connect to,
be it Joe, Bob, Rick, Sylvia, or Sue.

To those whom him cannot see,
    invisible to them he has to be!
    Yet, his wings flutter warmly against their being,
    albeit, not seen with their own eyes seeing
    his wings of white, silver and glittering gold,
    he wraps around them in a warm love enfold.
    They feel a sudden calm descend
    from where, they cannot comprehend,
    he gives them from the dark some respite,
    filling their world with much needed light.

To those who see him as of the flesh,
    as his angelic being a body does enmesh,
    he speaks sweetly and softly of things
    which make his exquisite invisible wings
    flutter for joy, a scented peace bringing,
    with a sweet love their being brimming.
    These beings look on and behold,
    in truth what they are being told,
    a gentleman, calm, taking the time
    to bring healing and a love sublime.

When he leaves to go back home in his white Transit van,
    his wings fold neatly in, turning him back into a man.
    He smiles at the success of each assignment completed,
    heading home sometimes, somewhat depleted.

He hopes his neighbour is tucked up safely inside,
so that from her busy-bodiness he can hide
as shattered after a day's work he can be,
as all who love him, know and see.
Except for his nosy neighbour Mary,
awaiting his homecoming curiously,
she pounces on him as he drives back,
not excusing him or cutting him slack,
for the long day he'd pretended to be grafting in wood,
His angelic assignments fulfilling as he faithfully could.

Chapter 16

To My Sweet Mother

I love you mum, with all my heart
   it broke my heart when we had to part -
   My heart shattered into a million pieces fell,
   my new friend Despair, I got to know so well.
   It has come to visit faithfully over the years,
   unsuspectingly moving me to torrents of tears.

Despair's companion slowly and silently came,
   taking me to desolate dark places with no name.
   A desert, barren of lush terrain,
   in this place, I was not the same.
   There, for a full seven years I was left
   without joy, of life and laughter bereft.

A seven-year dark night of the soul prevailed,
   my deep peace shattered, my path waylaid.
   Anguish, agony, isolation - a grief hidden,
   my soul writhing in pain - guilt-ridden.
   I had to keep turning up, day after day,
   not knowing how to act or what to say.

On the outside softly smiling,
   on the inside slowly dying.
   I was not deliberately lying.
   But, I had to find a way to make it through,
   all alone now in my world - without you.
   And when peace back to me did come,
   sometimes it'd stay, I have to say, mum,
   and it would steadily beam and shine,
   at others staying for a very short time.
   A re-awakening slowly, but surely came,
   from a tiny flicker to a full flickering flame.

At long last I know you are here
   with every breath I feel you near,
   Grief's been washed away, slowly, tear by tear.
   A new way of communicating we have found,
   one ear honed to heaven, feet firmly on the ground.
   Our love for each other, now stronger than ever -
   living in the loving eternal - now and forever.

II

Part Two

The Playing Field

"Where shall we all gather?"
we ask as we come to play together.
"Shall we make it the swings?"
voice after child-like voice rings.

Chapter 17

By the River

In the silent stillness I sit
    with the heavens brightly lit
    on the riverbank on this day,
    taking in what comes my way.
    Golden rays on green leaves glistening,
    trees, flowers, birds, and I all listening,
    to the perfect symphony of creation,
    in its original sacred, divine fashion.

The sun's rays dancing dazzles my eyes,
    on the water's still surface, they jive,
    with a joy - everything is so alive -
    I sit awestruck, taking in the scene,
    not to do this, would be obscene.
    Leaves twirling, twig's teasing tingle
    bird's chirping - a cheerful jingle.

Boats make the still water ripple,
    like it's drunk too many a tipple!
    Instantaneously, the water regains calm

reminding me of an ancient psalm,
in which it is promised that by still waters we lie,
taken care of and protected, until the day we die.

On branches browned, birds sit and sing
with open hearts, their songs do bring
a chorus of heavenly angels' choir,
which one cannot help but admire.
A yellow leaf slowly and deliberately falls,
whispering my name, *Mary,* it softly calls.

I smile and enjoy our little game
with the innocence of a child - no shame.
I remember how we are told to be born once more,
so that our loving Creator we wholeheartedly adore
gratitude for life and its abundant creation,
coming to me in waves of gentle adoration.

The light and the shadow continue to innocently play,
their own subtle messages they would like to relay,
reminding us of the light which inside lies,
and that no matter how dark - never dies!

Sometimes it seems to be blocked
the door to its portal locked -
just like the sun hidden by a cloud
inside it'll stay, till out it's allowed.

Then, when the dark shadowy cloud is shifted
the dark blocking the light, is lifted -
iridescent lights shimmer and glimmer galore,

exposing beauty, joy, love and all of heaven's lore.

The soul ecstatically dances,
   as the light joyously jazzes
   within and without our being,
   darkness instantaneously fleeing,
   a beauteous beauty it makes unfold,
   like that seldom seen and rarely told.

Chapter 18

Whispers of the Oak

I walked along the fields briskly
   on a sunny autumnal day.
   The oak tree whispered in my ear,
   this is what it had to say:

"Come child, come child, closer, closer
   I love it when you walk past me
   you look in awe and wonder,
   seeing not just a majestic tree.

You look up ahead at my acorns
   as they hang so daintily,
   like little crystal chandeliers,
   is this what you can see?

My trunk ever so ancient
   it looks so big and strong,
   The wisdom that it's created
   to you and all, does belong.

I have gathered my wisdom wisely,
   years of silently standing in my field,
   observing all that's around me
   does Silence - Wisdom yield.

I watch quietly the comings
   and the goings of the birds
   singing like a heav'nly choir,
   their song surpassing words.

I listen to the lapping water
   the sound puts me to sleep.
   Lap, lap, lap a' lapping
   all the way to the creek.

The gentle breeze's sweet soft strokes
   I relish and hold very dear.
   For when her gentle blows caress me,
   all my worries disappear.

The autumn's wind wild whispers
   become very loud,
   when winter approaches
   with a crash-banging sound.

I stand tall as its cacophony
   deafening billowing breath
   blows fiercely through me
   sounding like death.

I watch death simply,

as my leaves fall,
it doesn't grieve me,
no, not at all!

For I do not believe,
but for sure know,
Death into life dances,
as spring opens its door.

New leaves spring forth.
Oh, how happy am I,
coming back to life,
with joy I sigh.

The Earth keeps me safe,
feet firmly planted
or my trunk, shall I say,
shall not be supplanted.

I wait for your passing
in quiet expectation,
my roots listen out
in joyous anticipation."

Chapter 19

At Warborough Green

At Warborough Green,
   a solitary lady is seen
   laying on a bench in the sun,
   being given a message to the Son from his mum:

"Dear Yeshua, Jesus, God's only begotten Son,
   Your long-lost mother has finally come,
   to be your mother readily once more,
   got her foot through that portal door,
   her heart's overflowing with love for you,
   for all You are and for all that You do.

Inside my being I carried you silently,
   You were formed there almost unwittingly,
   I loved having you deep inside my womb,
   The living Son of God, in a live-loving tomb.
   Your true nature and all ours wholly divine,
   my body a tabernacle, your host, all thine.
   I watch you grow slowly and delicately form,

I nurtured your being, before you were born.

It felt like I'd always known You from forevermore,
   when the angel appeared though, I wasn't so sure.
   Then as you slowly and silently formed inside me,
   the truth of what you are - and what I am -
   I could clearly see.
   I felt so much love, as inside me you grew,
   not only love, but a deep joyful peace too.

On the day you deemed to come out,
   around midday or thereabout -
   I laughed with every contraction,
   for labour at its inception,
   was not hard labour or a hard chore,
   heavenly assisted was Your birth, for
   as we know from millennia before
   You are the Son of The Father incarnated,
   showing us how evil can be decimated,
   You are the Son showing us how - The Way -
   to Your Heavenly Father-Mother without delay.
   It is now pertinent we all heed Your call -
   to regain our child-like purity as before The Fall."

Chapter 20

Musings for the Month of May

I rejoice jubilantly in the month of May,
   the most beautiful one, I would say -
   to have it dedicated to *Mary. W*ho is she?
   Mary - Mother to all - wanting to be.

Flowers blossoming in full bloom,
   nourishing fresh fruits coming soon.
   Bright clear skies and the sun above,
   all beaming Light, Life-giving Love.

For the honour of what she is called to do
   for me, You and all of humanity too,
   I am grateful beyond words can express,
   my joy and thankfulness, I can't repress.

She has got grave responsibilities too …
   no-one be lost…. um…. or just a few,
   those who persist to shut their heart,
   pride and ego playing a perilous part.

The rest shall all come running to You,
   back in their hearts, your Love imbue,
   there may they stay forevermore,
   towards you rushing by the score.

Warmly receive them, each and everyone,
   "Come in, rest and have some fun,
   by special invite from Father-Mother-Son,
   we all celebrate – as we are all ONE."

You are the ultimate sacred space holder -
   Chaos, fear, disharmony are not of you,
   yet, You hold us within with so much love,
   calm compassion peace and playfulness too.

Chapter 21

The Wedding

I watch from a distance the wedding today,
  as I can't be present in any other way.
  It would've been lovely to have been there
  but, I am here, I can't be everywhere.

This celebration of love touches the heart,
  as this couple promises from love never to part,
  they promise to reflect on Earth, God's love
  and to be as divine below, as is sacred above.

Healing each other through life's ups and downs
  smiling gently through life's little frowns
  not taking themselves ever too seriously,
  relishing in each other, the other's mystery.

Allowing each other the free space
  to be themselves and not erase
  that what, who they are - unique -
  celebrating the other's wondrous streak.

Humility is key.
    It is not just *me* -
    We celebrate our unity,
    in a Life-Love-Light trinity.

A blank canvas new
    Love's paintbrush's hue,
    the couple slowly paint
    a picture simple, quaint.

They are able to reflect
    God's love, not neglect
    reminding humanity of values lost,
    bringing them back, "Ah x'gost!" *

Through thick and thin,
    without and within -
    May God bless this unity,
    in time and eternity.

*In their native Maltese language it rhymes with lost and means 'such joy'.

Chapter 22

Shine the Light

I touched evil this weekend
   in its rawest, most visible sense,
   Evil's anger, ego and fear
   with peace and love dispense.

I saw the face of evil
   contorting, looking *graceful*,
   a pretense to fool, beguile.
   Isn't this so disgraceful?

What is described as evil
   is what it's always been
   able to influence thought forms,
   camouflage what's plainly seen.

The power of illusion to deceive,
   the pure of heart contort,
   Reality, it has the hidden power
   to insidiously distort.

Evil shape-shifts, hides, misguides
   as it works covertly, underhand,
   open your eyes to see,
   so you can understand.

Once you get its game,
   and the hang of all its rules,
   activate your own light power,
   so you're not taken in as fools.

Our light-power is so potent,
   we forget how subtly strong,
   in silence, dispelling darkness,
   exposing all that is wrong.

You have the power to manifest,
   you have the power to fly -
   you know I AM, and you are too,
   In My essence does your being lie.

You have the power to see clearly,
   You possess the gift to know
   your soul-purpose, as you journey
   wherever you are, wherever you go.

Access your innate power,
   the darkness do dispel,
   use your own sacred light,
   so that all evil you repel.

If your light is not hidden,

but on tall lamp-posts exposed,
then darkness doesn't stand a chance,
it is straight away disposed.

The greater the evil,
the greater the grace.
allow your light to shine,
its luminescence embrace.

Hidden in the depths of hearts,
forever there it's been,
allow it to shine right through,
the brightest you've ever seen.

Evil hates the bright light shining,
it makes it painfully disappear
like an agonised wounded beast,
feeling and knowing death is here.

Connect to the light within,
allow it bright to shine.
Believe in your divinity,
My light is also thine.

Chapter 23

Drop it!

Drop the labels, the names, the shames,
  Drop the boxes, the boundaries, the games,
  the pigeon-holes - minds locked up in cages,
  conditioned - held hostage throughout the ages.

Drop the judging, the analysing - drop it all -
  Don't be scared, you shan't falter or fall,
  without these props that keep you going,
  making you think you have the knowing.

Wisdom comes from deep within,
  in the silent solace free from din.
  It does not come from the conditioned mind,
  but from a compassionate heart, you will find.

The heart an oasis of truth, stillness.
  a state of wholeness - no ill-ness.

Wisdom over aeons slowly forms,
base metal into gold transforms.

This alchemy, the human heart knows well,
let those who know, come forth to tell
of this subtle transformation of the heart
Sacred Spirit's and our own subtle work of art.

Chapter 24

WEAREONE

Love's always here to sustain,
   in you, it'll always remain.
   Do not fret or be afraid,
   The son-daughter of love you are made.
   Enjoy the rest of your Earthly sojourn,
   until I return, until I return!

The angel of doubt is near,
   do not lend him your ear
   for he comes to confuddle, confuse,
   your attention, him, you must refuse.
   Shut your eyes and turn away,
   Lest your will he tries to sway.

Trust in your new connection strong,
   nothing can now really go wrong.
   Things might appear strange and weird,
   don't be afraid – nothing's to be feared.
   For as I promise, so shall I perform,
   My Word is Truth, this is my norm.

My presence, My sacred essence's forevermore,
  you've now come in through the portal door
  to My kingdom of heaven, here on Earth
  as your heart is bequeathed a brand new birth.
  With one foot in through the portal door,
  you needn't be scared or worried anymore.

Mistakes are mistakes no more
  as I, your Creator looked and saw
  your heart so full of Love, so
  any *mistake* that you do make,
  I change into a blessing, for your sake!

It's beautiful how grace all transforms,
  into Love - creating new norms
  and ways of being are procured,
  new ways of seeing - secured.

A new heaven inside you silently sings
  its sacred music within joyously rings
  melodiously reverberating throughout
  your face, eyes, ears, feet, hands, mouth,
  proclaiming My unconditional love -
  in your third eye; a consciousness above
  the mind's fluctuations and its busyness,
  above all grief, despair and wretchedness,
  dissipating all your blame and shame -
  enveloped in My sacred Love, in My name.

III

Part Three

The End Game

"How long are you able to stay out?"
I hear all my playmates shout.
"Up until it's dinner-time," I say,
as my mother's sweet call I must obey.

Chapter 25

A Human Heart

Here, I sit with nothing to give You.
   Here I am, with nothing to do.
   My new heart's like a road map,
   each and every visible crack
   representing a road I've been down,
   swimming, sinking or about to drown.
   Lurking in the water's essence,
   of good 'n' evil there is presence.
   A road map to show the rugged terrestrial terrain,
   at times weeded, manured, at others yearning rain.

It has been battered this heart of mine,
   but, through the mercy of Love divine
   it has been mended, and made into one,
   from all the shattered pieces, it's been done.
   All the paths within it show
   the grace of Love, thereupon bestow'd.
   Delicately put together in golden glue,
   the minute pieces and big ones too.
   All bound back together into a tapestry,

the artwork - of my own life's mystery.

I look at my brand-new heart to me given,
    I am told my wrongdoings are all forgiven
    I know my essential being's pure,
    radiating light and love, for sure.
    There is nothing left for me to do,
    but sit like a cow in a field and *moo*.
    No judgment, no blame nor any shame,
    no winning or losing, this is not a game.
    Just being in the present moment,
    no commentary or vile comment.
    Accountable only to my sacred Creator,
    basking in the love of my divine Maker.
    Trusting the process, in my DNA engraved,
    all wisdom within me silently safely saved.

The world has taught me to detest,
    who I am and all the rest …
    To be like this, and say like that,
    to be this thin and not be fat
    to have dyed hair,
    and lots of flair
    to always act as if I didn't care
    to value what on the outside lies,
    not value life, as time's flight flies,
    to give up my life to the State,
    not count the cost, at any rate.

This all serves the deep-church and state
    wake up we must, before it's too late!

Our life-force they feed off for their own empire,
our blood subtly sucked out - for like a vampire
their jagged teeth cut through our
unsuspecting neck,
transforming humanity into a
nervous bl**dy wreck.

I reject their shameless laws,
   all their mandates full of flaws.
   I cannot by their regs abide,
   neither can I my true truth hide.
   When in the end all's said and done,
   I pray, "God may your Kingdom come.
   And may it be here, as it is there,
   our beings beaming Love
   and Light everywhere."

Sacred Love's own protect and put aside,
   let them in pure sacred Light abide,
   do not let them go asunder,
   with evil blunder after blunder.

This sorry state of affairs
   since The Split, it occurs -
   The inception of the devil,
   procuring this prevailing evil.

These few verses aren't just for me,
   as I weep for a broken humanity,
   all unfolding before my eyes,
   all the untruths - all the lies!

I'm not sure what I'm meant to do,
   sitting in meditation, am I meant to?
   Not looking back at the past,
   at this lifetime, it shan't last.
   Neither looking at a future state,
   nothing's guaranteed, at any rate.
   Here I sit and watch and wait -
   Will this my lingering fear abate?
   I sit with no expectation,
   of any intended outcome,
   no sense of loss,
   no sense of gain.
   I just sit -
   with how things are.
   I sit with what is.
   I silently sit with this.

You are my all,
   in You I sit tall.
   As all is one -
   I sit in you and in everyone.

My body silently throbs,
   with an anguish which life-force robs.
   My soul silently weeps,
   with a sadness which deeply seeps
   into my veins, into my every pore
   into my gut, right down to my core.
   My heart cries a tear of blood red.
   "Why?" My broken heart sadly said.

"Because God's love and Laws have been rejected
　　without the love of their sacred God - dejected,
　　deep into the dark pit they go,
　　sinking low, low, low, low, low!"

There doesn't seem to be an end to my pain.
　　Is this part of my earthly motherly reign?
　　The honour is mine, yet the anguish is too,
　　do you feel it the same as I do?
　　Do you experience your being of joy bereft,
　　leaving you stark naked with nothing left?

It isn't how it should be, I know!
　　There should be joy wherever we go.
　　But, this is how it is at the minute.
　　I shall stay with it, and go within it.
　　Without struggling to let it go,
　　staying with it, letting it be so!
　　And when it's done its job - played its part,
　　I acknowledge and thank it - I let it depart.

It leaves an indelible mark,
　　on the map of my sensitive heart.
　　Each mark has a lesson to teach,
　　until the end of that class I reach.
　　The map's unending roads and lanes,
　　lead me to unfamiliar places with no names.
　　As I arrive, there I sit still,
　　I do not move, not until
　　each and every sensation within me I feel,
　　whether I sit, stand or humbly kneel.

It's so hard just being still
  with nothing to do, not until
  the sensations move
  with nothing to prove,
  to fix or improve.
  Breath bellows forth,
  from south or from north
  filling my lungs with life
  cold, cutting, like a sharp knife.
  If only I could somewhere hide,
  where fear and anguish subside.
  If only I could go inside,
  and in there rest in a perfection true
  where I am not judged, by me or you.

This self-judgement like a blood-thirsty bat arrives,
  my inner life-juices for itself derives
  it makes for itself its own delectable juice,
  its own life-force wanting to spruce.
  It leaves me feeling quite depleted,
  not quite so self-completed.
  Do I need to batter myself like this?
  Did I some crucial class miss?
  Wouldn't my being relish some compassion,
  to grow in love, joy and in life-passion?
  Wouldn't my being want some fun?
  Wouldn't it want to be one with everyone?
  Does it want to be battered and beaten,
  like a delicacy savagely eaten?

No, it does not - for self-respect I have got.

I know my own worth, as from my birth.
I know deep down I am worthy of love and respect,
for the whole of my being - its every aspect -
If only I knew this deep down at the core,
where fear and fear of fear, are no more.
If only I knew this at soul-level so deep,
then my self-abasement shall not make me weep.
If only I knew this in every pore of my being,
perceiving it clearly with my inner eye's seeing
then nothing and nobody shall hold the master key,
to my birth-right sovereignty, and life-long liberty.

Chapter 26

Innocence Lost

Friend, fiend or foe?
  This is what Lilieth would like to know.
  Did he fiddle with her son's innocence,
  under the guise of love - such pretense?
  Did his filthy f**king hands touch her
  son's delicate parts, or does she err?
  Was it to satiate his own lustful desire?
  She hopes his soul burns in an infernal fire.
  Did he deliberately undress her son
  from his innocence, for his own fun?
  His own self-gratification satiated,
  her son's embodiment repudiated.
  His menacing touch molests
  her son's intimacy, his being infests
  with fear, and an anger not of him,
  filling the son with his perpetrator's sin.
  Her son's being, like a silken robe ripped
  of his innocent purity, brutally stripped.
  Being made to feel dirty
  dodging his abuser's flirty

looks, which the son terrify
his vile acts, the son vilify.

How can that abuser sleep at night?
He must know what he does is not right.
When he lays his head on his comfy bed,
why can't it be on a bed of nails, instead?
When he dreams of oceans blue, far and wide,
why can't he hear cold prison bars, him chide?
Riding into them on a robust big black stallion,
wearing a satanic demonic blackened medallion?
And once trapped inside those four thick stone walls,
all his own clothing to the floor suddenly falls.
He looks at himself stark-naked, in the nude,
whilst others snigger and sneer, for like food
all of the other inmates want a piece of him -
Oh, sweet, sweet revenge, much sweeter than sin!
Avenging what he had consciously done,
to Lilieth's pure, young innocent son.

All the inmates look on wide-eyed, at his pathetic private part.
Pointing at it mockingly and jeering - it was no work of art.
This thin small rubber-like cylinder, like a seed,
controlled his lustful appetite, fuelled his greed.
It would not yield fruit juicy and deliciously messy,
yielded only rotten dried up crops - nothing fleshy.
His delirious desires of the flesh, flare and arise,
from lustful satanic subtle temptation, I surmise!
For the flesh is pure until
demons are invited in. Still,
abiding in that greed and lust

flamed stronger, by gust after gust
of wind, that bellows the fire,
of lustful, sinful, wild desire.

In this prison cell comes an abasement strong,
  almost matching what he'd done wrong.
  The inmates, violent to the core,
  the upper hand he has no more.
  There is now no innocent child,
  with whom to go sexually wild.
  There are only inmates gagging,
  their tantalising tongues wagging,
  as this newbie stark-naked stands,
  whilst Satan, with his red-hot iron brands
  his name, on his servant's body exposed,
  as into this devilish hell he's being deposed.
  The piping-hot brand violently instilled
  a wrath which his vile being filled
  with anger, jealously, lust and greed,
  which now full-grown, no longer seed,
  are the fuel that spurn his every action
  from this evil, demonic, satanic faction.
  Inside the prison cell he shall stay,
  consuming meals of straw and hay.
  Behind the bars he does despair,
  his spirit dejected, his body in disrepair.

One by one, his limbs give way,
  dissolving into hellish fires, shall we say.
  His mind, it stays intact and sees,
  his body's misery as it wees

onto the cold prison cell floor,
just behind the locked prison door.
The stench fills the thick four walls,
as urine's condensed droplet after droplet falls
like a sickly yellow vomit-like rain, sticky,
all the other inmates taking the mickey.
How did he fall into such a dire state,
and of this prison become an inmate?
He catches a glimpse of his face, its reflection clear
exposes his evil-doing. I'm so sorry, my dear
son, for at his hand you alone had to suffer,
with no release, comfort or friendly buffer
to ease your anguish, or release your pain,
injected with fear, guilt and endless shame,
playing with your being, his satanic game.

You, just an innocent child,
loving life and running wild.
Innocently playing with your toys,
a little boy, who playing enjoys.
Indoors and in the great outdoors too,
sometimes alone, at others me and you.
My heart you filled with beauty and light,
our love for one another - sheer delight.
Yet, the symphony got rudely interrupted,
as your being was violently abducted,
by this evil force, inside this demonic man's heart,
to use and abuse completely, his plot's crucial part.

Now let's go back to the black prison stone walls,
where the cold floor suddenly falls

and gives way, like in a quake,
in which the whole prison does shake.
Suddenly, like a portal a hole opens up,
a vortex wide open, which cannot shut.

His heart sinks
   His breath stinks
   Death breathes
   Life leaves -
   His body bereft
   A legal theft.

He looks on confused, dejected,
   his being with fear injected.
   His feet lose their grip,
   on the crumbling floor slip.
   Deeper into the vortex he's sucked in,
   has he reached that place of sin?
   His body spins,
   as speed wins
   the battle of Time,
   paying for his abominable crime.

Swiftly and suddenly his feet give way,
   and his beaten body begins to sway.
   He seems to be quickly gathering speed,
   for security and stability he feels the need.
   But, deeper into sin he falls
   his body slowly, slowly crawls
   through a long, dark deep tunnel,
   which in parts narrows like a funnel,

he squeezes through to the other side
where fiendish groans and shrieks intensified.

Wishing in the narrow bit he got stuck,
   but, now he's running out of luck!
For you see, on the earthly plane,
   on others he vilely inflicted pain.
Now the tables have been turned,
   all his fun and frolics, adjourned.
He longed to go back, ask forgiveness,
   but, in this strange place he is,
dying to do another stinking piss
   and a sickening stench-filled fart
his most perfected work of art.
For the demons within had cursed his body to die,
   moreover, into this desolate stinking pit lie.
Here he is left empty, bereft of all,
   nothing is there, nothing at all.

He suddenly wishes he were dead,
   avoiding this hellish state and instead
of anguish, and a loss of control, he'd be,
   singing with the angels in heaven happily.
Oh! What had gone so suddenly wrong?
   Why is he not humming a happy song?
How has it all come to an abrupt end -
   and where shall these demons his soul send?
He had been Satan's loyal and faithful trooper,
   always lost in a lustful drunken stupor.
Is he now being punished for a loyal servant to have been,
   faithfully following the precepts of Satan's satanic scheme?

Coercing, controlling, and destroying all that is good,
as a dark angel of Satan diligently should,
mocking and demeaning that which is innocent, pure,
making them, degrading lustful acts, silently endure.
He demands to know what is his reward,
as out of the funnel he heads toward
what seems like a bottomless pit,
stinking of urine, vomit and s**t.

The answer echoes booming, but the message isn't thwart'd,
as the crashing speed the sound vibrations contorted.
"You have had your reward already mate,
your greed and lust you did fully satiate
to the brim and overflowing -
subtly veiling your own inner knowing,
mostly through your own ego deceiving
believing a heavenly prize you're receiving.
And to those innocent kids through your teeth you lie,
as you strip them of their innocence and them beguile
seeking to corrupt them to the core
their beings violently crushed to the floor
feeding off crumbs from your sumptuous meal,
stomach churning, heart emptied, it's hard to feel
any love, warmth or even any affection,
procured by your evil satanic infection.
Just emptiness, the worst state of being procured,
your faithful service, Satan's dominion secured.
Of course, your soul now can't be spared,
as in this state, nothing can be repaired.
What you'd done, you knowingly and willingly had done,
at the expense of an innocent child, having oodles of fun.

You were warned early on, what working for Satan means,
your childhood teachings did shed light, spilled the beans.
So an excuse like 'I did not know'
shall not set you free to go.
Oh no! Oh no! Oh no!

If you think that this is bad,
  then I'm sorry mate, I'm sad
  to say, that there's worse coming your way,
  as in this hell you've chosen to come stay.
  You had been given chance after chance,
  to change the tune and the moves to your dance.
  So sadly for you, but not for me,
  You chose on this evil path to be."

The road to hell like a highway wide,
  most are tricked into driving on the wrong side,
  being taken in by the glitz and the speed,
  Satan's lustful ways they faithfully heed.
  Their egos fed, muffling their inner knowing,
  whilst selfishness, lust and greed are growing.
  Nothing is never ever enough
  of the base material, sexual stuff.

"With Satan, you worked hard to destroy what Love creates,
  poisoning the seeds Love sows, as It patiently waits
  for them to fruition finally come,
  pouncing on innocent daughter or son.
  He riled you in with empty promises sweet,
  and others too, whom, this same fate shall meet.
  The most dreaded state of being in His realm you shall

embrace,
    the state of being nothing - Nothingness - as you fall
    from Love's grace.
    To be in a state with nowhere to hide,
    your nothingness know, and in it abide.
    This is the worst state of being you'll ever know,
    your sins dancing before you, your mind them does show.
    You are rightly terrified at what lays in store,
    being denied the glories of Love's heavenly lore.
    You are scared of being nothing, so
    rightly shriek in fear, and terror know.
    What you dished out to boys and girls,
    comes to haunt you now. It all unfurls
    before your eyes, as you see your sin
    this time, this battle you shan't win.
    You fall deeper into the pit,
    clambering through stinking s**t,
    wishing you had chosen a different path,
    to avoid this hellish aftermath.
    Yet, many would agree and rightly so,
    this state of hell, you deservedly must know.

You made innocent others suffer at your hands,
    concocting evil and shameful plans.
    You forgot that one fateful day,
    you shall in a state of hell lay.
    One from which there is no respite,
    no wings for you to take off into light,
    escaping this Fate that you have chosen,
    leaving the souls of many dead or frozen.
    Your evil before your eyes shall forever beam,

into an infernal eternity, it does seem.
There is nobody to come and save you here,
your position I'm making currently crystal clear.
The desecrated bodies of those children made sore,
shall procure your own punishment, and what's more
shall be calling to you from their place up above -
their beings restored - as white as a dove."

+

Chapter 27

USED AND ABUSED

POET

The world is currently upside down.
Trying to smile - instead I frown!
Tears strolling down my cheeks
my whole body shakes, my spirit weeps.
Why is this happening to us? Oh why?
I can hardly breathe, let alone sigh.
Why, oh why, won't we open our eyes -
Call a spade a spade, and untruths - lies?
Why are our hearts so closed to care?
Why are we not loving - don't we dare?

Stinging darts
Broken hearts
Shattered dreams
Silenced screams
Angered anguish
Non-spoken language
Sighing breaths
Brutal deaths.

God - sacred eternal Life - unconditional Love - infinite divine Light reverberating through sacred cosmic Sound; mainly, an experience beyond any name, label, description or humanely constructed concept.

"When my children come back to me,
　my passionate love for them they'll see.
　Return to My heart of Love and know,
　All My Love on YOU, I yearn to bestow.
　I cry watching you all suffer so,
　My love not wanting to know.
　Your bodies for fodder used
　your embodiment used and abused... ."

POET
　...for someone else's wild wiles
　whose depravity beguiles,
　Freedom silently stifles.

The Abusers – The Cabal, The Elite – deep-state; deep-church and any person who has abused their position of power and people's trust – abuse can be physical, sexual, verbal, psychological, or emotional. The abuser thrives on secrecy, secret societies, secret agendas and will torture and kill those who whistle-blow or go against their flow. Those who do, are the martyrs of our time.

They prey on innocent children's blood,
　their narcissistic ego they fully flood
　with the need to coerce, control and destroy -

104

by means they can overtly or covertly employ.
Their weakness exhibited,
their love non-existent
their private parts minute,
their whole being destitute.

Their insides rotting, vile
their lungs all the while
exhaling poisoned air -
but, do they care?
The evils within them smile,
appearing *sweet* all the while.
A heart made of stone,
room for self-love alone.
Their eyes dart out hate,
poisoned words, their bait.
The children young, get stung
laid out naked, alone hung
on a line of deception,
for at its inception -
evil
lies
its foundation -
deceit
to defile -
an innocent child (or adult, or nation
or the whole wide world).

Justice is coming, it's on its way.
They'll all be made accountable, come what may.
The last judgement is near.

They shall face it in fear.

The Abused - **All of us (referred to as child/children) who have been manipulated and coerced into submission, our sense of child-like innocence, duty, loyalty taken advantage of; manipulated into obeying edicts which are not for our highest good, ones which feed fear and sow division. It happens on an individual level as well as on a global level, as is now and has been throughout the history of humankind.**

Their return long-awaited,
    Anger, fear, now abated -
    as closer to themselves they draw
    seeing this is not their fault or flaw,
    but the debasement of their abuser
    vile, defunct, f**king child-user.

The child knows that they are pure within
    that their whole being is free from sin.
    They recognise that this is abuse,
    to face it squarely they don't refuse -
    They tell themselves once and for all:
    "I must tell – it's my shout, my call.
    I will explode if I keep it all in,
    It needs to come out what lies within.
    I need to verbally and openly express
    my sense of shame and unworthiness.
    I wish someone would listen without any judgement,
    see the coercion, manipulation - its not called abuse

for nothing! It was always so damn'd hard to refuse.
Seemed at times there was no way to say "No".
I carried the shame and the guilt so
nobody would know.

Through that mental torture, bodily shame,
  I feel like a person without a name -
  Obliterated is the sense of who I am, you see,
  I feel as debased, defiled and dirty as can be,
  I shower for hours, but the dirt seems to stick,
  I've had to protect myself with a wall made of brick.

I was always told if I were to tell,
  the bell of death - its every knell,
  would ring inside my parents ears,
  a swamp of blood and a pool of tears
  would overthrow my mother in despair,
  a state so shocking beyond repair.
  My father would believe me not,
  for heart intelligence he has not got.
  He would disown me as defiled,
  he would say that I have lied.
  A way out there was not one
  it's OK for you and for some
  others, who have not been abused,
  for others' amusement have not been used.
  It's not so bad for such a one,
  you've got a life, I've got none!

This shell I inhabit in darkness and fear,
  I don't like others getting too near -

107

lest they smell anguish and touch my pain,
I must not let them this vantage point gain.

So in my everyday life I'm in complete control,
  for when my abusers the deadly dice doth roll,
  I have to dance to their tune, perform on their cue,
  the rest of the time, control is my due.

I think I control what I do, how and when,
  outside the iniquity of their soulless den.
  I put most of that abuse aside,
  deep in my psyche, I let it hide.

I hope that buried there deep within
  away from full view, it rests therein.
  I am on constant guard lest it comes out,
  and in full throttle it begins to shout:

<u>The inner voice of Truth</u> ushering forth from within where it's all been buried deep, hidden, now ready to be exposed and freed from the tyranny of secrecy and silence.

"'Of my innocence you have robbed me
  slain myself, till all I can see
  is a shadow of the being I am meant to be.
  Like a thief you have left me bare,
  I cannot go anywhere
  where this shadow doesn't go,
  where f**king shame doesn't show,
  where control consumes, fears abide,
  a state of being in which I can't hide!

My being - my being no more!
  You're in like a thief through the back door.
  Your scheming ways full of lies and deceit,
  a crossroads where evil, a psychopath meet.
  You offer me money, toys and expensive treats,
  you buy me delicious meals and unusual sweets.
  I don't care for these artificial goods, empty things,
  I'd much rather be given a strong set of wings
  to fly away every time you come near me,
  saying money is power, as you enter me, you see.
  You say I enjoy it as much as you do
  and if I say no, you say ... ."

The Abuser - **The manipulation of the abuser – sometimes subtle, at others much more overt - will go to any lengths to get its own way through control, coercion, deceit and lies.**

"... you know I'll tell who!
  Your mother or your father, or preferably both.
  Would you like to encounter your own father's wrath?
  Or would you like to face your own mother's disbelief,
  as you openly disclose and sigh a sigh of relief?
  They won't take your side, they won't believe you,
  you could say I'm family and they love me too,
  I'm always welcomed through the front door,
  don't you dare speak up to settle the score.
  Don't you dare tell our secret little child,
  if you know what's good for you, hide!
  I'll deny it all till I'm blue in the face,
  you'll be called a liar and just in case

you're not scared of speaking out
I am the adult and I can shout -
louder than you. I have more clout.
You'll fail miserably if you decide to come out!
But, if you keep our little snide secret safe 'n' sound
pressies, holidays and much more shall abound.
You should never materially lack,
although your soul I have smeared black.
I have tainted and black-painted all of your being,
open your eyes if you can, I own your own seeing!
I dictate when we do it, how and when,
I decide what toys we use
as I now use and abuse
your body, mind, heart and soul
for my own amusement, my goal!

And you may want to ask 'why'?
I'll simply say it's because I can.
You are the boy - I am the man.
I call the shots and you bow down,
you are the slave- I wear the crown.
I will get away with this, you know -
nobody will get to know, friend or foe.
I control every aspect of this situation,
I end the session, as I procure initiation.
I am almighty, powerful and strong
you are little, powerless and always wrong.
I, of sound mind and of body too,
all that I say and do is always true.
You are worthless, but not when I call -
not when I ram you from the back on the wall.

You are so worthless, but not when we shag,
not whilst I thrust it all in a bag.
I am not insane, or mentally deranged,
it is the world that is changed! Oh so changed!
I am not evil, sinister or bad -
only a demon - you've been had!
I am not going to go to hell and burn,
as my abuse makes your stomach churn.
You are the one who'll carry guilt, blame,
I'll go scot-free, with a clear name.
No blame shall ever stick with me,
as I cover my tracks ever so carefully.
You are the one who will be shamed,
if you go public, you will be blamed,
they will think what a terrible thing he has done,
I hope that he's punished, that little piece of scum."

Poet

So as you can see -
    you, me and everybody,
    the abuser lies through his jagged teeth,
    manipulates, coerces, scares and terrifies,
    his behaviour with awful threats dignifies.
    Fear his currency,
    lies his warranty.
    The abuse is not just sexual,
    but physical, emotional and mental.
    They gas-light their shame,
    humanity's taking the blame -
    living in its contrived hellish kingdom,

111

being stripped of its sovereign freedom.

But, not forever or forevermore,
    for one day soon, they'll have to settle the score!
    All the defilement that they did to one and all,
    is what they will suffer themselves and much more.
    Whether here on Earth, or in a hellish hell,
    I am sorry to say which, I cannot really tell.
    But, as they did do to others, so to them it shall be done -
    They have defiled God's Daughters - abused Gods Son(s),
    the Law of Universe won't let them off scot-free,
    for Justice must reign, for peace to be -
    they shall be made to pay in full and more,
    and one day soon, they'll have to settle the score!

Chapter 28

The Playground

The symbol of the rainbow
   so drastically has changed
   and by this evil ruling cult,
   its meaning re-arranged.

It used to simply symbolise
   the covenant between God and Man,
   nothing will ever come between them.
   Do you think it ever can?

Not so our own evil,
   not any less our *sin,*
   can ever keep away God's love
   from flowing forth within.

For inside - our very essence,
   is the infinite spark divine,
   the greatest gift we're gifted,

allow it bright to shine.

Not to control, consume or worse destroy,
   but, to enjoy our brief earthly sojourn
   in these playing fields we freely roam,
   playing and dancing while we learn.

For joy is the highest of vibrations,
   it lifts up all those who,
   come over to the playground -
   everyone's invited - you are too!

The swings a wind of joy create,
   their motion to and fro -
   everybody can freely enjoy,
   you needn't be a pro.

The thrill of the slide as you sit at the top,
   just before you simply let yourself go,
   whooshing down at neck-breaking speed,
   Life's worries away blast billow and blow.

The merry-go-round reminds us all
   that *what goes around comes around*,
   making all so deliriously dizzy and
   not everybody's cup of tea, I found.

The tall trees in the playground,
   protect both old and young,
   as they unite in having fun,
   their songs not left unsung.

For the shrieks of joyous laughter
   ring in the playground's air -
   filling it with love and joy,
   spreading swiftly everywhere.

It's sad to see a playground empty,
   no children being allowed in.
   The gravest of our century's travesty,
   the gravest, greatest deadly sin.

Replacing the children's fun and laughter
   is a lifeless poster of a rainbow in colour,
   substituting fun and life in the playground,
   Emptiness fills it like no other.

So sadly now the rainbow symbol - rife and everywhere -
   as you go in and out of shops and everywhere you stare,
   a symbol of death and darkness, it has suddenly become,
   as the Cabal, the Cult, the 1% control the whole world as one.

The colours shining bright on paper, are still - lifeless - dead,
   as sadly kids playing in the playground, are being made to
dread.
   We adults - protectors of our children have a lot to do -
   We must set our children free, without much further ado.
   In saving our children from this treacherous tyranny,
   we'll be saving ourselves too, you see.

So, get off that sofa and *subito**, smash that beastly black box.
   Summon all your strength and courage, and the cleverness
of a fox.

Empower your free will, call on your creativity, open your
mind too,
bring the children back to the playground and bring yourself
- yes, you.

Don't give your freedom and breath away to an evil elite,
who you and the whole of humanity gravely mistreat,
they've taken the symbolism of the rainbow, making it to
mean
dying and death -
taken our children, our freedom, our livelihoods -
and lastly, our life - our breath.
Do not comply, do not consent, do not acquiesce, say no!
Do whatever it takes, to make this evil go.

An end to this we must procure,
and we must do it soon,
for this evil plan as it unfolds,
is the whole playground to ruin.

We must act fast, we must act now
tomorrow might be too late,
as they barricade the playground
locking up its front and back gate.

Do not comply, do not consent - unite together as one ...
This is the only way we can once again have some fun ...
This is the only way this silent war is going to be won ...
And now having strongly willed it - so it shall be done.

*subito - Italian for straightaway.

116

Chapter 29

THE END GAME

It seemed like a dream,
but what does it mean?
Who can explain to me,
so that I can turn the key
unlock its significance -
Is it deliverance?

DOMINIC

A solemn, secretive young lady in black,
surrounded by black front and back.
A long black coat to the floor she wore,
I'm sure that's not all that I saw.

Her long, straight black hair
was pitch-black, dark, not fair.
It almost swept the dark black floor,
matching the black coat she wore.

I could only see her back
as she stood there clad in black

slim, sullen and tall -
I suddenly hear her call:

"Get those scissors, as I tall stand,
    for this hair - please understand,
    needs to be cut short -
    most of it, I must abort.

And this long fur-edged black coat,
    hanging on me like a dead goat
    drags me down with its weight,
    it shortly needs to meet its fate.

Come, quick this coat do cut
    short, shorter, and that door do SHUT!
    Lest a draft enters this room -
    or a ray of light, as it's morning soon."

The servants hurried to the door
    suddenly appeared by the score
    to execute her raucous orders,
    they flew in, from across the borders

And from across the miles -
    All straight-faced, serious, no smiles.
    A harsh demeanour all exhibited,
    as a cold reality they all inhabited.

They were all getting ready for war.
    The Queen - their sovereign saw
    that her claws hadn't as yet sunk in

to a planet not far from *Sin*.

Sin is the planet she took over
    for she was very, very clever.
    The name of her planet an outdated word,
    made for her a powerful strengthy sword
    with which to enslave whom she can
    namely every woman, child and man.
    She would want them all for her own,
    across the galaxies this is widely known.
    She appears only to those when
    her other *enemy* Satan's den,
    is overflowing with iniquity,
    which it has been since antiquity.
    They used to be buddies him and her
    but, he did gravely, gravely err.
    Taken in by her beauty,
    he underestimated her strength.
    She, on the other hand, would go to any length,
    to outsmart him and lead him astray,
    then to *Sin* she flew away.

There she set up shop and stayed,
    plans went swiftly, nothing delayed.
    All her drones quickly followed,
    the old planet emptied, hollowed
    executing on *Sin* her sinister plan
    to control, consume and destroy all she can.

In working against Satan, but with the same aim
    she didn't realise (as clever as she was)

that they played the same game -
and though being on opposite sides it seems,
both were pulling together in sordid dreams.
The two forces joined strongly as one,
the fierce war on humanity 'd begun.
They joined together those two forces,
their reign of evil on Earth enforces
fear, anger, jealousy, terror to no end,
the rules of God they break and bend
crushing the precepts of the Laws of Love
they would be in charge as a One World Gov!

These plans they hatched from many aeons before,
to strip humanity of its heavenly lore -
to decimate the sacred Earthly Mother Divine
for this, their secret evil plan they had to refine.
For the Divine Earthly Mother was so wise,
from their actions she did quickly surmise
what their evil plans are -
to put an end to them, and bar
this destruction, she will do her very best to try
with a weeping heart, which with grief doth cry.
Will her children heed her warning
as she shouts from the rooftops every morning
that afoot are evil plans, to destroy them all
as they'd lost their paradise after The Fall?
Will they her divine Wisdom heed?
In warning them, will she succeed?

Some people she planted on magic soil,
that which they tilled with timeless toil.

They all got savagely murdered - dead -
Their Spirits silently on that sacred land tread.

Others like Earth angels delicately clad,
   full of grace and love - it's been said
   were scattered all across the land -
   by mountains, forests, sea and sand
   to be beacons full of Love and Light
   and with their flame of Light blight,
   the darkness that'd possessed the Earth,
   stripped it naked of all fun and mirth.

These too were destroyed,
   their minds 'n' spirits deployed
   to serve Dominic's sinister plan
   as evil hi-jacked them as it can.
   For vigilant they were not -
   naivety and ignorance they'd got
   tricked into evils' illusion of light,
   their luminescence dissolving, with evil blind.
   Not clever enough to outsmart her in black
   her army, which eventually came neck-to-neck
   with these Earth angels, warriors of Truth and Light
   fighting fiercely to take their dimly lit light in a fight,
   of Good against Evil as from all time -
   She openly declared: "They are all mine."

She secretly knew
   this was not true,
   for she knew the power of Light,
   Its strength, its forceful might.

For she had once been of the Light too,
but beguiled by Satan's traps like many, not a few
she fell for his illusion hook, line and sinker so,
Light and Love's power she clearly did know!

Yet, her allegiance to the Beast she swore,
always black attire she wore -
her demeanour sour, her sustenance fear
feeding off it - wide and near.

MARY

Suddenly seemingly out of the ashes she rose,
For The One in Black thought her dead, I suppose.
Alas, actually sojourning the Earth she had been,
the most beautiful Lady, the purest you'd ever seen.
Soft, pale, shining skin -
to pink porcelain doll skin akin,
draped in a silken satin elegant white gown,
from head to the white marble floor down -
hung flowing like a waterfall'spath clear, pure,
matching her sweet, serene, simple demure.

She stood straight 'n' tall facing her fairy-like, lush garden green,
arrays of colourful flower beds, butterflies and birds as ever
seen.
Fairies tended this magical piece of land,
dazzling angels lent them a helping hand.
She would melt hearts with her loving smile,
authentic, simple, true – not out to beguile.
The sun accentuated her clean compassionate heart

metamorphosed silently into a sacred work of art,
not through playing evil games
nor by buying into illusion's ways,
as her opponent Dominic had done
hoping that, that way the war'd be won.

No, Queen Mary of Heaven as many would attest,
subtle manipulation, coercion and control 'd detest.
Yet, to understand fully her own children's plight,
down to Earth she descended, with them to fight.
She was there in person amidst the cruel madness
carrying in her heart an overwhelming sadness,
over how far humanity from sacred Love 'd strayed,
not in divine and sacred Life-Love-Light had stayed.

She watched it all slowly unfold,
the greatest story still to be told.
The outcome still not made visible,
to proud and evil hearts, incredible!
She suffered as she held her anguished children's hand,
with love and compassion, broken hearts she'd mend.

For their suffering was her unending pain -
since the murder of her Son, she was never the same.
She had her own questions, her own brokenness too,
the same as me and the same as you.
There was a lot of healing, that's true,
that Queen Mary of Heaven, had had to do.

The path she chose of the meek and humble
made black clad Dominic crack, crumble;

for Dominic couldn't understand why
this Queen so simple and sometimes shy,
gentle – sweet soft smile – all the while -
would win for Heaven's side many a heart and mind,
guiding them back to themselves and to God, you'll find.

Her orders she did not bellow or bark -
she would simply pray and with a heavenly hark,
entreat the conscious power of Father-Mother-Son
to silently and sweetly come back to life in everyone,
so their innate Life-Love-Light divine they may know,
and the deep-seated peace and joy it doth bestow.
Once their hearts and minds awaken – they shine,
their Beings like heavenly choirs' ecstatic music chime,
waking up Consciousnesses that had been there,
silently sleeping,
now dispelling the phantom-like illusion
that they had been keeping
and as in a dream-like state, duly doped
awakening them inside, Queen Mary hoped!

The heavenly chime woke them up, dispelling darkness,
their awakened consciousness perceived the starkness
of the bright luminous Light now uncovered,
their true identity divine sacred rediscovered.
For they had known all along who they had really been -
Dominic and her troops as illusion were now being seen.
As clear as day it suddenly became crystal clear to all,
that Dominic and her troops had procured The Fall.
Jealous of the gloriousness of divinity in human embodiment,
Dominic and her troops fought, and would not relent

to drag humanity down into their dark gruesome hell,
its embodiment transmuted into a sickly sordid shell.
But could she win this battle, really?
As the divine Conscious Spirit within,
destroyed it cannot be!

So, Dominic et al had cleverly created the Illusion -
    Many sadly fell for her deadly delusion
    and believed all that they were told,
    that their bodies were empty, they didn't hold
    divine Love - Consciousness supreme -
    manifested in and through a human being.
    This suited Dominic and her troops to a tee
    and in so doing all her troops and she,
    would manipulate, control, consume and destroy
    these divine beings believing they were just a stupid toy.
    It was such a clever plan -
    and things for Dominic were starting to pan
    out – until …

The still …
    soft whisper of sacred Love inside,
    decided silently it will not hide
    anymore. It would shout out loud,
    the wind of its sound vibration moved every cloud,
    which each Being's clear blue sky had blocked -
    When this happened – Dominic et al were shocked.

For the sacred Love within now fully awoken -
    the whispers of Truth clearly within spoken,
    showed beyond a shadow of a doubt

in its simple stillness, no need to shout,
that every life-form of the true God of sacred Life has come,
and in and through Its Infinite Consciousness all this begun.
A live Light Conscious awareness vibrating with Love,
Its heavenly sound vibration filling below and above,
everywhere and every live being,
use your own inner mind's eyes, seeing,
your own and all of creations divinity
there is no God out here or only there,
God is within you and everywhere!
The experience of our higher Being, this I,
is what makes us Divine and that's why,
it is easy to mistake God and soul as two
when all is one, Divine Consciousness and YOU!

Dominic and her evil troops want us all to forget
    this is our Truth, our higher Being they don't want us to get.
    For this Truth, Dominic et al are fully aware of and know
    is what shall wake up humanity from its slumber and show
    up, all else as insidious illusion,
    Dominic et al as deadly delusion,
    who wants to appear as truth,
    I think a little bit uncouth!

Truth will show how as God they dressed up,
    in their frenzy to deceive, they wouldn't shut up!
    People will perceive how hard to trick they had tried,
    how through their rotten teeth to us all they had lied.
    Their plan to brainwash and coerce these untruths on us all
    trying of sacred Life, Love and Light to muffle the call,
    is now coming to a sudden close and soon

Dominic et al shall face their doom – BOOM!

Chapter 30

Epilogue

It is post the Year Twenty Twenty -
Children playing everywhere a' plenty,
filling up the fields and playgrounds,
laughing merrily on the merry-go-rounds.
Relishing ice-cream cups 'n' cones by the score,
happily sliding down slippery slides, galore.
Swinging high up in the air,
shrieks of laughter everywhere.
Children joyfully playing in groups,
from near and from afar like troops
who are celebrating their victory
over years of treacherous tyranny.

Most adult-like beings had stayed sadly asleep.
The children knew that *they* life must keep
going, and living according to their own Light,
fighting for their freedom with all their might.
To begin with it was very hard -
not a glimmer of hope – not a shard.
Yet amongst them a child-like grown up said:
"This is wrong - DO NOT CONSENT –

We must rise up instead!
We must not stay in our bubble or square,
be the day rainy or be the day fair.
We must not keep two meters apart -
not the size of a bus, nor the size of a cart.

We must look at each other with wonder and care,
summon our courage and we must dare
to go against these evil edicts which stop
our freedom, and our life-force crop!"

The *children and other child-like adults* listened intently to this
and seeing that their own family and friends they all so miss,
decided to heed this child-like woman's call
to put an end to this tyranny once and for all.

They sadly saw their parents are still fast asleep,
knew, that the light a' glowing *they* must keep.
Life was disappearing fast from the planet – oh, so fast,
they must act quickly – before the last
remnants of uncontaminated air disappeared,
and the Earth of pure air is deliberately cleared.
The *children* knew that deep, deep inside
the little voice which inside likes to hide -
Echoed the words of this child-like woman with hair
which made her look like a big brown grisly bear.
Yet, her heart kind like that made of gold,
in all fairness – this must be told.
They all began to pull together as one -
To save humanity, *their* mission 'd begun!
'Twasn't *Save the Children* campaign - it was not.

It was the other way around, as children had got
what it takes to set enslaved grown-ups free,
and so it was, *Children Save Humanity*.

They summoned their courage like a loud lion's roar
as how humanity needs them, *they* very clearly saw.
Their parents fast asleep, needed waking up soon,
otherwise everybody would be facing their doom.
In their bubbles they decided they would not stay,
face the consequences they would, come what may.
They would not stand two metres apart -
"What good would that do?" they asked for a start.
These were *children and child-like adults who* urgently needed
to play -
needed to hug, dance, skip and jump in abandon without
further delay.
Although in many these urges had been wiped out,
there were still enough voices who started to shout:

"All you adult-like beings out there, you should all be ashamed
at how controlled, fearful and gullible you are -
you've all been framed!
These random measures to keep you so much further apart,
edicts which from sovereign freedom, life and love depart.
These measures to wear a mask on your face -
a symbol of slavery on your face, you embrace.
The vaccine, part and parcel of the plot and the ploy,
dehumanising your being - you is not a stupid toy.
The nano-tech which is imparted within it,
will your mind and body control and inhabit.
In the end you wouldn't know whether you're coming or

going,
   this is the end of all your seeing, hearing, feeling and knowing.

We children from across the world united in will shall be -
   as this predicament of you sheep-walking adults we see.
   You are doped up on sugar and sickly sweets,
   eating junk food and gorging forbidden meats.
   Innocent animals being murdered for your whims,
   these are on you – their deaths – your sins.
   We, the *children* are eating well and very healthily,
   as how you've ruined your health we so clearly see.
   We, the *children* shall save your precious lives
   lived in honey-deprived hexagonal bee-hives,
   that have been built to enslave each and every one.
   Step out of it now, quick! – Your liberation's begun.

We are awake and for goodness' sake
   forge forth, you all free to make.
   Free from the tyranny of slavery
   admire our bravado and bravery
   and join us unanimously
   as we fight forcefully and tirelessly,
   to cut these fierce fetters which bind -
   procuring freedom of soul, body and mind".

So like the pied-piper of Hamlyn, the Woman played her flute .
   The *children's* voices who followed were loud, not mute
   they could be heard from east to west
   and north to south, as all would attest
   to hearing their voices loud and clear,
   whether relatively far, or whether quite near.

They danced, skipped and jumped whilst they sang,
as their voices throughout the Earth's ends rang.

They reverberated throughout workplaces, offices, schools,
through playgrounds, shops and outdoor pools.
Their singing was incessant and did not stop,
heard in every street corner and corner shop.
Some dressed in white and others in blue -
they came to wake me up, and yes, YOU!
A child's gentle call waking you up from slumber
gently nudging you, and hoping you remember,
that you need not be afraid -
nor into a subservient slave made.
And if this gentle nudge is not enough
then *children* are made of tougher stuff
and would form choirs of different symphonies
waking up your minds, souls and lifeless bodies.
They were not going to give up and cease,
in the name of an artificially concocted *deadly* disease.

A fear of death children have got none.
Although some adults sadly in some
did put the fear of death into their offspring -
their bodies alive - silently and lifelessly sing
the song of the wretched reaper,
scared to death – that as their Keeper,
He would come suddenly to gather their *sinful* soul,
fear and fear of death, these deluded parents' goal.
Sadly, passing on fear ignited by the State,
many adult-like parents to this did relate.
The fear spread from parent to daughter or son,

like wild fire it spread to almost everyone.

Some *children* were spared and what a relief,
    as their power to fight's been beyond belief
    these are the ones following the woman,
    there is one thing they all had in common -
    the innermost voice within, hadn't been muffled
    their minds, their mouths had not been muzzled.
    Thanks to some child-like grown ups who an open
    mind 'd kept
    and in the chaotic confusing current state of affairs,
    hadn't slept.
    But, tirelessly and ceaselessly worked to awaken
    at great personal expense - do not be mistaken,
    for easy it had not been -
    but worth it as we have seen!

For these *children* entrusted to save humanity now
    altogether in the playing fields gathered somehow.
    It is thanks to *them* that evil regimes suddenly fell,
    joyful knell, after joyful knell of a peaceful bell
    heralding freedom, justice, life and *their* victory
    how it all happened – the greatest mystery.

Fetters falling
    Voices calling
    Bars breaking
    Earth's quaking
    Cells decimating
    Spirits rejuvenating

Finally, evil melts into obsidian oblivion.
  Freedom, Life-Love-Light rule – no division.
  A child-like being, its faith and power triumphant over all -
  What would we've done hadn't our *children* heeded the call?
  What fearful Fate would humanity had faced,
  had her *children* their headstrong heads not raised?
  What would've become of her sleep-walking sheep,
  hadn't it had *children* a watchful eye on Truth keep?
  What would've happened had these *children* been had too,
  and wouldn't have been able to wake up me and you?
  What if these *children* hadn't heeded the call,
  deeming they were insignificant – too small?
  What if the last shreds of Life in *them* had been destroyed
  and their life-force to this end had not been deployed?
  Luckily for us all – these *Children* saved Humanity -
  from enslavement, imprisonment, death and tyranny.

Divinity in a human embodiment ethereally veiled,
  Its Word – through child-like beings is revealed.
  Out of the mouth of innocent babes,
  adult-like beings awaken in waves!
  A voice is never too small,
  to proclaim the message to all.
  Waking up sleeping adult-like beings divine
  who live and act like hellish beasts who dine
  on egos and illusions far too big to care or see,
  their broken, fallen Humanity,
  having lost all its dignity.

  .

  We must heal this division
  Free ourselves from this prison

Uncover the lies,
Answer the *why's*
Question the State,
before it's too late.

Finally fully awake they are now,
saved by their children somehow.
Truth within them opens its eyes,
Sacred Life-Love-Light within like the phoenix rise.

About the Author

Born to Maltese immigrants in Australia in the 1960's, Mary sailed back to Malta after her fourth birthday with her parents, leaving her grandparents behind. The abundant joy of both families reuniting was in stark contrast to the bad turn that Mary's mother mental health had taken over those years. Mary cared for her ill mother till she took her own life on the 20th December 1993. It had been a harrowing journey, yet one shrouded in unconditional love transcending time and space, giving Mary a deep insight into the human condition. This is depicted in Mary's latest publication https://books2read.com/b/4EJ6QO – Liberation at Last by Mary Mallia in December 2023, an epub commemorating the thirtieth anniversary of her mother's passing.

In 2017 whilst visiting family in Malta, Mary started writing poetry. The poetry written and published so far has stemmed from a lifetime of soul-searching, reflecting deep spiritual experiences and self-reflection spanning decades. Mary explores themes like the meaning of life, death, suffering, injustice, abuse, light, dark, healing, empowerment and enlightenment all thrown into one.

She currently lives in South Oxfordshire where she enjoys walks in the luscious countryside and a living-room with a river view which has inspired a lot of her poetry. Writing is her passion and has been since her teens, but she also enjoys dancing, yoga, meditating, cooking, baking, entertaining and socialising. Mary is also a British Wheel of Yoga trained Yoga practitioner and teacher, as well as a healer.

You can connect with me on:

🌐 https://www.marymallia.co.uk

📘 https://www.facebook.com/mary.mallia.148

🔗 https://www.youtube.com/@marymallia5744

Subscribe to my newsletter:

✉ https://www.marymallia.co.uk/contact

Also by Mary Mallia

A Return to the Heart of Love

This anthology of poems invites you to rediscover and reconnect to Love's sacred essence. It is that which resonates across universes, whilst lying at the heart of your being - mind, body and soul. This unconditional Love empowers you to live in harmony and equanimity with yourself, nature, Mother Earth, and all others, for optimum physical, mental, emotional, psychological and spiritual health and well-being.

This collection brings together Christian and Buddhist philosophies and practices echoing wisdom accrued over millennia fostering human growth, expansion and enlightenment. The lingering impression is one of sweet peace and contentment, reflecting the transformative power of Love.

Liberation at Last

Amy, having taken her own life just before Christmas and her daughter's engagement, finds herself in a state of being which is a far cry from the rest in peace she had always hoped this would bring her.

Her biggest challenge here is to confront herself and her previous life without despairing. Has she got what it takes? And will others still on the physical realm of existence have the power to hasten or delay her release from this limbo she finds herself in?

Printed in Dunstable, United Kingdom